My Handwriting Word Book

Grades K–1

Donald N. Thurber

Scott, Foresman and Company

Glenview, Illinois   London

Good Year Books

*are available for preschool through grade 12 and for every
basic curriculum subject plus many enrichment areas. For
more D'Nealian® handwriting practice books and other
Good Year Books, contact your local bookseller or
educational dealer. For a complete catalog with
information about other Good Year Books, please write:*

Good Year Books
*Department GYB
1900 East Lake Avenue
Glenview, Illinois 60025*

1314 VIK 98

ISBN 0-673-38477-2

Contents

Introduction

This book contains many of the key words children will use in kindergarten and first grade. Also listed are all the words from the kindergarten and first grade D'Nealian® Handwriting programs, including the difficult "wh" and "th" words; day, month, and number names; and all the two-letter words. In addition, there are extra pages for writing special words the children wish to remember. These can be any of the hundreds of words used in daily conversations.

Teachers may wish to copy the pages and have students make a notebook. Children might, for example, collect class spelling words, classmates' names, field trip words, or words used in science, reading, and language skills.

While riding in a car, children could use this book to list names of things seen while traveling. Items from home, play, and special events are other sources of collectible words.

A good learning goal would be to try to fill the blank pages by the end of grade one. Children like to discover, write, and save certain words, creating their own personal vocabulary.

Parents, grandparents, sisters, brothers, or teachers should help spell unfamiliar words for the writer. Six- and seven-year-old-children *should not* be expected to correctly read and spell all the words listed. However, these are many of the words they will encounter and should recognize by the end of the first grade.

It is wise to remember that children grow and develop at different rates, and that since girls mature faster than boys, they usually develop their writing and reading skills earlier. Boys catch up later!

The parents' job is to keep children *interested* and *motivated* to learn. Being positive and encouraging the children will bring large rewards in the learning process.

How to Teach the Letters

a — Middle start; around down, close up, down, and a monkey tail.

b — Top start; slant down, around, up, and a tummy.

c — Start below the middle; curve up, around, down, up, and stop.

d — Middle start; around down, touch, up high, down, and a monkey tail.

e — Start between the middle and bottom; curve up, around, touch, down, up, and stop.

f — Start below the top; curve up, around, and slant down. Cross.

g — Middle start; around down, close up, down under water, and a fishhook.

h — Top start; slant down, up over the hill, and a monkey tail.

i — Middle start; slant down, and a monkey tail. Add a dot.

j — Middle start; slant down under water, and a fishhook. Add a dot.

k — Top start; slant down, up into a little tummy, and a monkey tail.

l — Top start; slant down, and a monkey tail.

m — Middle start; slant down, up over the hill, up over the hill again, and a monkey tail.

n — Middle start; slant down, up over the hill, and a monkey tail.

o — Middle start; around down, and close up.

p — Middle start; slant down under water, up, around, and a tummy.

q — Middle start; around down, close up, down under water, and a backwards fishhook.

r — Middle start; slant down, up, and a roof.

s — Start below the middle; curve up, around, down, and a snake tail.

t — Top start; slant down, and a monkey tail. Cross.

u — Middle start; down, around, up, down, and a monkey tail.

v — Middle start; slant down right, and slant up right.

v

Middle start; down, around, up, and down, around, up again.

 Middle start; slant down right, and a monkey tail. Cross down left.

 Middle start; down, around, up, down under water, and a fishhook.

 Middle start; over right, slant down left, and over right.

a A

a

about

across

add

again

and

another

April

are

around

as

ask

at

August

away

ant

apple

NAME

b B

backwards

bag

ball

bar

be

bears

bed

bee

been

below

between

big

boat

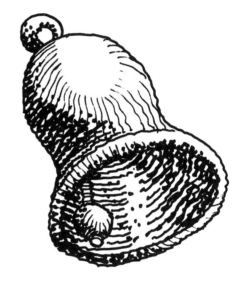

bell

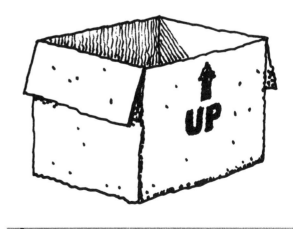

box

NAME

4

c C

call

can

case

cats

cave

cheese

children

close

cloud

coat

cod

come

could

cross

curious

curve

cow

cat

NAME

d D

dad

day

days

December

did

do

does

dog

dot

down

draw

drink

deer

door

NAME

e E

even
every

each
eat
egg
eight
eleven

ear

elephant

NAME

f F

fall
February
find
fine
first
fish
fishhook
five
flowers
fly
flying

follow
food
for
found
four
fox
Friday
friend
from

foot

From My D'Nealian® Handwriting Word Book: Grades K–1, Copyright © 1989 Scott, Foresman and Company.

NAME

g G

get

girl

give

glad

go

going

good

great

green

grow

gymnastics

guitar

grapes

NAME

14

h H

had	him
halfway	his
hand	holes
has	horse
hat	house
have	how
he	
hens	
her	
high	
hill	hammer

NAME

16

i I

I

if

in

inch

insect

into

is

it

ivy

igloo

NAME

j   J

January

jet

job

July

jump

jumped

jumping

June

jar

jug

NAME

20

k K

keep
kind
king
kitten
kitty
know

key

kite

NAME

22

_l L_

love
looked

land
learn
left
leg
letter
library
likes
list
little
long
look

leaf

leaves

NAME

m M

made

make

man

many

March

May

me

mean

men

mice

middle

milk

Monday

monkey

more

move

moving

Mr.

much

mud

my

moon

NAME

26

n N

name

new

nighttime

nine

no

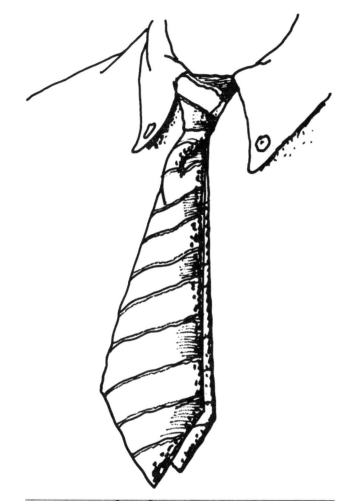

not

November

now

necktie

nest

never

nut

NAME

o O

October
odd
of
off
oil
old
on
one
only
or
other

our
out
oven
over

owl

octopus

NAME

p P

paper	play
park	please
part	pull
parts	
people	
pigs	

pail

pig

NAME

q Q

queen   quick

quilt

NAME

r R

rabbit

ran

read

reads

ride

right

ring

river

roof

rug

run

rooster

robot

From My D'Nealian® Handwriting Word Book: Grades K–1, Copyright © 1989 Scott, Foresman and Company.

NAME

36

s S	
sad	shoes
said	six
Saturday	slant
school	so
sea	some
see	squirrel
September	start
seven	starting
shadow	stop
she	Sunday
shells	snake

NAME

38

t T

table
tail
take
than
that
the
them
then
these
there
to

this
those
three
Thursday
top
too
Tuesday
tummy
twelve
two

ten

From My D'Nealian® Handwriting Word Book: Grades K–1, Copyright © 1989 Scott, Foresman and Company.

NAME

u U

us

use

used

umbrella

uncle

under

until

up

upon

umpire

NAME

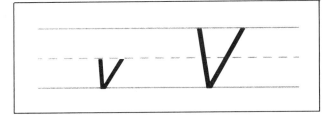

v V

vacuum

Valentine

vase

very

visit

violin

volcano

NAME

w W

was

water

way

we

Wednesday

well

went

were

what

when

where

white

who

why

wig

will

wolf

word

would

wagon

From *My D'Nealian® Handwriting Word Book: Grades K-1*, Copyright © 1989 Scott, Foresman and Company.

NAME

46

x X

x ray

box

next

ax

exit

NAME

y Y

yes

year   you

yellow   your

yo yo

NAME

z Z

buzz

zipper

zoo

zero

zebra

NAME

52

Two-Letter Words

an	he	no
am	hi	of
as	in	oh
at	if	on
ax	is	ox
be	it	pa
by	ma	so
do	me	to
go		we

Number Names

1 one	13 thirteen
2 two	14 fourteen
3 three	15 fifteen
4 four	16 sixteen
5 five	17 seventeen
6 six	18 eighteen
7 seven	19 nineteen
8 eight	20 twenty
9 nine	30 thirty
10 ten	40 forty
11 eleven	50 fifty
12 twelve	60 sixty

70 seventy

80 eighty

90 ninety

100 one hundred

Animal Names

Places I Go

Names in My Family

58